The Islands Project

~

The Islands Project

Poems For Sappho

≈

Eloise Klein Healy

🐓 RED HEN PRESS | *Los Angeles, California*

Book design by Mark E. Cull

ISBN-10: 1-59709-085-9
ISBN-13: 978-1-59709-085-8
Library of Congress Catalog Card Number: 2006936789

The City of Los Angeles Cultural Affairs Department and Los Angeles County
Arts Commission partially support Red Hen Press.

Published by Red Hen Press

Acknowledgements

I would like to thank the editors of the following publications in which several of the poems appeared, some in slightly different versions: *Black Clock 6:* "Sappho's Fragments"; *COLA 2005 Individual Artists Fellowships Catalog*: "Wind In Mytilene"; *Electronic Poetry Review*: "Memo: Folk Art 101"; *Feminist Studies*: "For The Girl Child," "Sheena, Queen Of The Jungle, Lived"; *Ms Magazine*: "Hardscape"; *Prairie Schooner*: "Artemis To Aphrodite," "The Elements"; *The Los Angeles Review*: "Rites"; *Nightsun*, Issue 25: "Flower Shop"; *Poemeleon: A Volume of Poetry*: "What I Would Want To Know"; *The Women's Review of Books*: "My Mothers," "The Isle of Echo Park"; *Writers At Work Postcard Series 2005— "What's Cookin?"*: "Recipe With Dogs."

"The Grackle On The Lawn" appeared in the "Bird Exhibit," L/A Atrium Gallery, University of Southern Maine, Spring 2007.

The portion in italics in "Greek Rhythm With Greens" is from "I Can't Stop Loving You" –original lyrics and music by Don Gibson, Knoxville, Tennessee, June 7, 1957.

~

There are many people whose generosity of time and spirit were crucial to the writing of this book. I want to thank those who were helpful readers: Robin Becker, Tara Ison, Carol Potter, and Terry Wolverton. Special thanks to Colleen Rooney for the hours listening to these poems. I am also grateful to the translators of Sappho's work, particularly Mary Barnard in whose book *Sappho: A New Translation* I first met the poet. To Anne Carson, utmost gratitude for the clear window to Sappho and the inspiring comments in *If Not, Winter*. I wish to thank Judy Grahn for her book *The Highest Apple* that set me thinking about my own project, and Page du Bois' book *Sappho is Burning* for engendering questions in me about how to approach Sappho. I also want to acknowledge and honor and memorialize Arlene Raven, feminist art historian and co-founder of The Woman's Building, for her workshops on lesbian artists.

I wish to extend special gratitude to the Department of Cultural Affairs of the City of Los Angeles for an individual artist fellowship—The COLA GRANT—awarded to me in 2004-2005, that allowed me to travel to Lesvos. I would also like to thank the faculty, staff, and students of the MFA in Creative Writing Program at Antioch University Los Angeles for their unstinting support of my work. Similarly, I am grateful to Mark Cull and Kate Gale of Red Hen Press who continually amaze me with their tireless efforts as publishers. Their friendship sustains me, as well. During the writing of this book, my mother, Carmen V. Klein, died. I miss her support and love every day.

This book is for Colleen

someone will remember us,
I say, even in another time
—Sappho

Table of Contents

The Islands Project

The Islands Project

With so much open ocean,
I'm glad for any land at all.

Hardscape

Say it's the memory of early mornings
in the shop, the power lift raising a car
in the dawn light, steam lifting off the highway
in front of the garage, and tools
coming to life at the touch of a hand.

Say it's the clang of things, the ping
of ball bearings pouring into a pan
and then a gush of gas from the pump,
the cleaning rag running over
the steely marbles to spark their shine.

Up the hill, the farm horse's shoes
tap against the gravel on the road,
the tack clinks and groans, the barn doors
bang and creak and corn stalks screech
against each other in the wind.

Say it made me hanker for hard things,
want to get outdoors first light, handle sticks
and dead tires, bang old mufflers together
and bam a ball peen hammer
against a scrap of sheet metal behind the shop.

It made me not want dolls and the demands
of indoors—quiet in the parlor, quiet by the stove.
It made me a woman of landscape and weather
and suspicious of my place. Say it gave me
a chrome handle to a different and difficult world.

The Grackle On The Lawn

She wants the blossom.
She wants the seeds in the grass.

She wants the beautiful thing.
She wants to eat.

It's so simple, she's like a person.

She wants the beautiful thing.
She wants to eat.

She's like a person, she wants to live
with that beautiful blossom and she wants to eat.

She flies off with the blossom in her beak.

Audacious

How dare I speak
for Sappho?

How dare I say I
know the intention
in her line?

I say I know a door
when I see one.
I know cattle on a hill
and a cup of wine.

I know how an afternoon
is made and then tips
into evening.

I know a gesture carries
fire across time
and I know she
meant to speak to me.

How do you know what
Jesus meant except
feeling the words
pierce your heart,
align with your breath?

I Know The Word Is Figment, but I Think "Fragment"

I know the word is figment, but I think "fragment"
of the imagination, something other than the whole, a piece
whose outlines are supposed to fit somewhere, but now is an isolate—
as in *a language that is the only known surviving member* (a scrap)
of its language family — and whistling into the wind like a bit
of music or a song lyric made up on the spur of the moment

but never to be, never to be sung to anyone. That moment
could be an island too, a magnificent outcropping of rock, fragment
of a chain moving away from its source, bit
by bit, carrying from its fiery birth core pieces
of emotion. Then a shoreline gathers around it where scraps
of other moments gather, build the isolate

into a homeland, an anti-isolate
that lives on as more than just a moment,
and each tide carries to it more than scrap
metal lodged in wood, plastic bottles, shell fragments
and miscellaneous debris. A random rescued piece
becomes a better bit

when joined, when each bit
meets its neighbor and the isolate
is shown to be a rich piece
of an unfolding archipelago, a moment
in which feeling extends and shows that fragment
is form, that sea floor or heart-scape (scrap

of paper/poem) is never just scrap,
never limited to being the tiniest bit
of a life, but that every papyrus chip, fragment
of marble, tooth or rib, footprint in mud, isolate
for centuries is still as alive as its original moment
when that piece

sits next to the right piece,
when what was considered scrap
without its twin is instead like a moment
expanding in memory, replaying like a bit
of a song, when the lonely isolate
or broken note sings like a soul's fragmented

tongue for a moment, it chimes in mind, a piece
that shows the fragment is not a scrap,
not a bitter lover, alone and disconsolate

Sappho, The Essential Shape

We're essential shapes
sitting at a table in the library,
between us stacks of books.

I hear you breathing.

Between us sits the Bible.

I hear you breathing.

Leaves on the trees
twirl in the wind.

Between us Jesus
and the few things he said
twisted into those iron laws.

I hear you breathing

and each breath makes
you *you*,

minute to minute
the forever possible
reaches across time.

Dots on mulberry paper
are leaves outside the window,

are trees in the petrified forest
on Lesvos,

trees made of stone,
the living things
their own museum.

I hear you breathing
across time
in the burned libraries,
in the muffled gestures,
in the prohibitions.

You and I are alive
though the prohibitions came down
whole against me.

Breathing,
you and I are alive

Wind In Mytilene

and on the waves in turmoil
in the harbor
gulls floated
like pieces of paper
set adrift, little
boat-like birds
twirling
in the wind-tossed waves
that drove into
the strong arms of the seawall
at the apex of the bay
where a statue of Sappho stands,
young woman
with a lyre—not
looking out to sea
but glancing at the curve
of the seawall
and the birds,
those lost notes
before rain

Arrival

I am living in a lineage of desire
defined by others before me.
It's why I've come to walk the beach
at Skala Eressou and follow with my own eyes
the curve of Sappho's horizon
defined by the sea and the headland
on the western coast of Lesvos
where small waves rock and rise
and rock again.

Nothing is as real as place or the words
for a place and how the world sometimes
bursts open with what cannot be explained,
like the the gray January day I arrived
at Sappho's beachside town.
I parked in the one parking lot
and made my way through the tiny streets,
all the buildings shut
and newspapers pasted over the windows.

No one. No one walking about.

Just a bonfire burning on the sand
and a poet arriving to see for herself.

The Living Fragments

for my mother

Her sentences broke verbs into bits,
her syntax shards of a time sequence
shattered in a swallow.
Some foreshock drug had pushed
a verbal precipice to slide
and dive to insane depths.

"When did I go crazy?" she would ask.
She wasn't crazy. She had many minds.
They all made sense, just like a word
on a fragment of papyrus means something
even when you know the rest are missing.

My mother would think I had children,
that she was cooking a roast, that dad was still alive,
so our conversation often ended up
like Scrabble in zero gravity.

It turned out we could talk about the Dodger game,
the Laker game, the spring flowers out the window.
Unbelievable that she and I were able
to piece together what she cared about at all.

So I read Sappho's fragments
with a trained eye. She is my other
blasted heritage, beautiful
in disarray, the aftermath
I didn't have happen
right in front of my eyes.

Wrapped in Sappho's Words

Wrapped in Sappho's words,
a mummy comes down to us
in its vestment of papyrus.
The dressers couldn't have known
how to place the scraps of the poem
in sequence or align its music
to the frame of the body.
Knowing only the time signature
of eternity, they'd reached for what was at hand
and plentiful, the reeds of the river
and centuries of wind.

Artemis To Aphrodite

The Parthenon—East Frieze panel #856
Apollo, Poseidon, Artemis, Aphrodite

OK, I know about the sparrows
in the dust, the storm of their arrival,
or love like a storm of arrival
and a flight of birds.

I'm the one supposed to be the hard lover,
but even with your sweet smile
and winning ways,
even with your promises
and devotion,

look here—
my arm stretching to touch
your shoulder,

you've made it stone
where a moment ago the folds of your garment
were running grass and
you were turning to greet me.

The Singing School

I saw one narrow as a blade
in a man's black suit

I saw one drop her pages
on the floor and walk away
from the microphone like a bullfighter
turning his back on a bull

I saw one with generous breasts
in a floral print dress
shift from one foot to the other
while her body blushed all over

I saw one in pain, in pain
enough for ten strong women
but she didn't say a word about that
pain, she went deep under the water
and came back and she wasn't alone

I saw one who's breasts were cut off
and she sang anyway saying,
"Nobody cut my throat yet"

I saw one who mid-wifed the language
of her tribe and taught everyone
to dance to its music

I saw one comb through history
sifting the dust for rings, for broken links
of gold, for altar pieces and the altars, too,
for the shapes of animals and birds
in conversation and divinity in the tracks of deer

I saw one in her coffin strewn with roses
and lilies, the narrow heaven she made
rising around her perfumed and dense as diamonds

I saw them in their labor and I saw them laugh,
and all of them, all of them have passed down Sappho's street
in Eressos and stood at the beach
where the dark rock stands, where if you look carefully
you can see a lioness about to rise and go

Understanding Sappho The Musician

Most Like	_Least Like_
Laura Nero	Emily Dickinson
Patsy Cline	Elizabeth Bishop
Lady Day	Sylvia Plath
Janis Joplin	Jorie Graham

Tutelage

for Sappho

I must admit I didn't think of you
when first I fucked a woman who had given
birth. Before, I'd learned with green and grassy
girls who clenched with furious delight my tongue
or thumb or fist. But this was a room in
another room, a world behind the walls
where men don't go, or if they do they fall
into the fear of capture. I fell, too,
but enraptured by the flesh of it all.
And taking me in, she took me too far
in my mind, she took me out its door, she
who only hours before had pulled my shoulders
through her car window, kissed me on the street.
Gripping me like life or death, she said
she wanted me to fuck her hard and harder
than I ever had and did I understand?
"Of course," I said. Of course, I lied or
only later knew the cost of truth.
Tutelage means you'll learn. Tuition, you pay.

How Much Can I Have Of Sappho?

I

Which fragment gets to be mine
and what empty room
where you imagine I possess her
at last? Where I wrap her
in an embrace?

Sad and limited, that view,
when I intuit she and I would be rivals
with our eye on the same woman.

II

What can I have?
I already am what's missing.

It's a complicated embodiment
I'm after. Meaning. Snapshots from my life
need to be rearranged on pages
and linked in a timeline
like papyrus chips
put back in order.

Or video clips I've saved to DVD.
Here's one in a winter landscape.
Two women meet at a street corner
under bare trees, a threatening sky.
From here, we see gestures, some talk.
Then, they clasp each other tight
like old friends might, except
there's a minute change in the angle
of the hips. Not friends touching
shoulder to shoulder, but lovers,

deeper, deeply touching the full length
of the body, the pelvic circle of heat
you can feel burning from here.

III

I live with the anger that Sappho and I
are denied each other.
She's a word like "aunt," I'm a word like "quaint,"
we're always off-rhyme,
two words like "ain't."

People say to me, "You know, she didn't have to be
a lesbian. You know nothing
is proven, right?"

A one-size-fits-all meaning of the word *lesbian*
is one I don't even ask for.

"What would Sappho think?"
I ask myself. She would think, "Who's that
new girl?"

IV

People just can't find
a way to let me
have her.

And why not?
What would they
lose then?

Maybe people just feel a need
to put me in my place,
to set me straight.

The Lyric In A Time of War

for Sappho

Let my music be found wanting
in comparison
to yours (as it must)

let me be found loving
(as you were)
extravagantly the beautiful

let me find you
and the song (forever)
between us

in these terrible times

The Isolates Aswirl With Life

she is water all
around me
rocking against
my thighs
there's a little fumble
in the float
until our hands
touch

the gods don't really
mind except to note
with praise
how close
to divinity she is
and how I worship her
with such care

Self-Portrait As Young Eros

"A woman who loves a woman is forever young."
—Anne Sexton, "Rapunzel," *Transformations*

I was sitting in the back seat,
being driven to the airport, when
my friend's husband turned to me
and said, "There's an adolescent energy
in your new love poetry. What's that about?"

That was about 25 years ago. Newly out
of my marriage, out-of-the-closet,
I knew what he meant. I'd exchanged
my old clothes for a rocket suit.

There was an aura of the orbital
in my behavior, as if I was looking at my life
from space, and simultaneously turning out
to face the stars from a new angle.

He should have known what that felt like.
I had just stayed overnight
in a spare bedroom in their house,
On the computer screen, when I went to bed,
was a small spiral, and when I woke
a whole galaxy he had plotted
was spinning slowly across a grid in the background.

"It's a new world for me," I had told him.
I already knew I would have to be sixteen
again for awhile. And then eighteen
and twenty-eight and thirty-two.

But like young Eros, I would always
be on the brink,
my fingers pursed around an arrow
like a kiss.

Why I Call On Artemis, Not Aphrodite

because there was no hearth
because there was no home
because there was no place or position

at the barricades
at the defense of the clinic
at the staging area

before the cameras arrived
before the demonstrations
before the broadcasts

in line for the signs
in rain and wind outside the building
in constant phone communication

where the buses embarked
where the flyers were printed
where the marchers gathered

doing the paperwork
doing the fact checking
doing the scheduling

because we were women
who met in the time of struggle
and loved in the alleys of ourselves

and fell to our knees in our knowledge
and fell on each other in thirst and hunger
and fell into love in an endless time of war

A Kind of Exile

I

We're safely camouflaged as just two women
ambling toward the boulevard on a walk,

except there's the carload of teenage boys
to think about, their arms waving,

their heads sticking out the windows
as they turn the corner, hell-bent

on speeding down our nondescript street
hoping to terrorize the locals.

You can feel the two-second lock
of the gaze of the one who gets it,

who yells out "Fucking dykes!" in a tone of voice
that muddles between announcement

and threat. The crowd at Starbuck's
scans the street, too, as the car speeds off. Who? Where?

II

The street, the emblem of the public world,
long contested turf where not just lesbians,

but two women by themselves don't belong. Of course,
my neighborhood is benign

as the milk and cereal in a suburban bowl,
except the car might be circling the block.

It doesn't take much to go from *there*
to a very bad *here*. How many times

we've looked back to locate
just when a confrontation got nasty.

At least, it's not night. There's a Maytag store
just around the corner, and a chiropractor we know,

and it's the twenty-first century, right?

My Mothers

for Alicia Ostriker

My voice has three mothers,
my own mother, Carmen,
and Sappho,
lost in history
for different reasons
but both preserved in me.

I heard in my mother's voice
the inflections of her family,
my old Montana uncle
and the stones of the White Rocks
up where the Missouri River is born.

My mother in later life would fade a little
as evening came on,
her tone of voice shifting to Uncle Roy's
as if she had tuned into
a radio station on a long trip
across open country.

And Sappho I hear with my eyes closed,
the push of a woman
singing into my chest,
thrilling as the hum of my mother's voice
when she sang to me as a child.

Whitman described it best—the "valved voice"
Where would I be without Walt?
Mother Whitman, as Alicia calls him.

Sometimes my Freshman English teacher
made light of him, the words "handkerchief
designedly dropped" and "my barbaric yawp."
I sat through the class, rehearsing poetry, knowing
in an inchoate way
what it would take
to sing in a woman's voice

as maybe Walt tried to do,
or maybe he just tried to sing
and a woman's voice joined him
from the soul of the world

The Elements

Fire for anger, water for change,
earth for stability, wind—well,
who knows what wind is about?

In life, they mix so.   Like that day
I was taking a shower
with my girlfriend and she told me

she was sleeping with
her ex-lover again. Wasn't
a fire supposed to leap

out of me, or wasn't water
there to drown the flames,
or wash her clean of betrayal?

Wasn't the hillside out the window
there to settle me, inform me
of the underlying design
and long term balance in things?

Wasn't some wind going to blow
those words away and leave us
soapy and sweet smelling

in that shower, just about to
towel off, have a drink,
cook dinner and read a little?

Wasn't my love for her supposed to mean
I could step into the same river
over and over again?

Sappho's Fragments

Maybe someone else
is responsible
for them or

maybe she threw away
all the poems
about men

Maybe she grew tired
of the missed meetings
the lame excuses

maybe just maybe
she had had it with
love lyrics she occasioned and

her bed empty at dawn

Maps of Things Relatively Permanent

the color red   a blush that rings the cheeks
the sun at dawn   the sun at sunset in the west
the flush on the upper breast

the beautiful moon a sleeping lover
surprise at distance   at closeness
the silver lawn shadow-less at night

a robe   folds in fabric
hillsides deeper green after rain
the textures of linen and flax and cotton

horse   the tail flying straight
round muscles and flat muscles
the wild eye and the tame eye

wine in cups the grapes solidly present
seasons changing but holding back
taste that stings then softens

longing for the good
invincible emptiness of loss
then a gesture with the palm up

The Day After Meeting Her

In the fourth year of my marriage
and in my parent's home
and in the little den
that had been my writing room
while I was in college,

I sat down and began
to make a history
of my sexual self

and there was always a woman there.

None of the words
was unfamiliar to me—
incense, apples, groves of trees—
or the catch in my breath
when a woman sang a song.

But the fragments reconfigured.
Puzzle pieces moving
in three dimensional procession
were proof instead of excuse,

and in the fourth year
of marriage, my heart froze.

I was somebody else
to myself than the woman
who the day before
had gone to visit a friend
near the beach
and turned at the sound
of a voice
in the doorway.

A woman was standing there
in the way there had always been
a woman there—
incense, a catch in the breath,
the image of trees meaning love,
a list snapping into place,
fear that I might already know
what I was about to know.

This was in the fourth year of my marriage
and the year of my first book.
It was in the summer.
I went to the beach and back again.
I took off my clothes
and shook inside because

she was there
and there had always been a woman
in me

looking for her

The Isle of Echo Park

Rainstorm, nowhere
to go.
I've got a husband at home.

She and I meet at Barragan's
and walk a half a block in the rain
to my car, outpost or haven,
who knew then. It felt
dangerous as hell
to be out
there in a steamed-glass cage
with White Fence gang bangers all around.

But we sat in my fogged in
fogged over car,
an island in a rising sea
of late-night traffic, high tides slamming
down Sunset Boulevard
east of Echo Park Lake.

That the island wasn't in the lake
is what I would reference here.

Bathed by a gulf stream of feeling
that rocked and lulled me into thinking
I was swimming, not drowning,
I was being ferried cargo and caravan
to a different shore.

What flag was flying?
Who was the pirate?

And where

did I think I was going that night?

Sappho, You Must Have Had A Mother

who died,
who slipped out of your life
and for awhile left you
with little to say,

and in that time,
did you have a daughter yet
who also cried and held onto
something your mother gave her?

I carried my grandmother's rosary
in the left front pocket of my jeans
for years. Just yesterday,
I took it out of the old jewelry case
grandfather gave me.

There was a bead missing
that I hadn't noticed before.
The wood of the cross was worn
and the silver of the cross was worn
so that the thin body of Jesus
liked like a shadow instead of a man.

When your mother died, did a ritual
move the grief through you
in the way it is said ritual does?

I don't have the kind of faith
I once had, so I find it's better
to think on the bead that is missing
and think of silver and wood
slipping through my fingers.

Flirt

"Lesbia quid docuit Sappho nisi amare puellas"
"What did Sappho of Lesvos teach except how to love girls"
—Ovid

I only flirt with
you because Sappho can't is
what I tell myself

If There Were No Books

Where did you two girls
find time
and place
to be alone?

And if you couldn't bend
your heads over a book,
lean into and laugh
with each other,

how did you
touch
by accident,
and then because you wanted to?

One Poet To Another

I see you got a Guggenheim.
I see you sold my book online.

I bought it back and now it's here—
my signature addressed to "dear".

Reclaiming makes us square at last.
We're even now, oops! not so fast—

that lover whom you took from me
in Venice, fall of '83.

The Sapphists

So what if they all throw
like girls?
They catch
like girls do, too.
Taking in, whole-body pressing.
Catch in the throat
just thinking about it,
something inside me
saying, "Safe, safe at home."

So what if they run
like girls?
They're never caught
like girls, picked off
or stuck in a run-down.
No, they keep their eyes
on the ball,
and when you're not looking,
a little spit on their fingers.

Love Poem From Afar

for Colleen

I

This morning I'm more lonely than the sky,
that flattened tray of tin and rain

before the robins' quick array of ruddy breasts
displayed the air a way that's new

as when in their noisy gang
they flew against the blue

like stitches in a quilt
that's being aired out with a shake.

I take some solace watching starlings
with their yellow bills root among the leaves.

They're plump with some success, those clerks.
Field notes, perhaps, or a survey of the seeds.

II

Your day still sits under the horizon
while mine unfolds in steps I take
to make myself familiar here:
breakfast in the kitchen, carry tea upstairs,
keep a careful list of birds I've seen.
Tai chi, before or after.

I know we're on the same planet,
the same sun coming in the east window.
I know how and why time zones float
like gauzy curtains across the globe.
But here's the fact that sends me to the page.

I want to see you every day we're in this life,
mark change with you as we change, as we age,
for it's true, as you say, it took a long time
for us to find each other and much pain.

Being away, I think only of telling you
about these birds, these swales of rain
and flowering trees so different from our own.

This would be another world
with you in it.

No—you are the world

Memo: Folk Art 101
To: Miss Moore
From: Eloise Klein Healy
CC: Miss Swenson
Miss Bishop

Miss Moore,

Let me introduce you to Folk Art 101
half-way across the road
and not yet noticed by my dog.

Could it be that coming our way
is a hayrick made of pine
and overstuffed like a sock monkey
or could it be a "slo-mo" voodoo doll
followed by an unlit fuse of tail?

No, it is the Goddess of the Night,
Ms. Opossum on a ramble
from the Laundromat hedge
to the trailer park bramble.

Neural equipment all small "n,"
she's sloped and shaped like a country wagon
rolling on four differently sized wheels
so she's slow to reach the median,
but her quick U-turn there
is based on a long history of danger at the double-line.

She is so ancient that when the tree fell
in the forest, she heard it
but did not hurry herself.
When Africa rammed Asia, she demurred
and turned to look at the sea level adjusting.

Behold your reaction, which until now was unschooled.
To the casual appraiser, she's a handmade muffin,
but she's pantheonic and mythic,
magical as Mardi Gras.

Her tail, you think a mangy snake, cools her down.
Unremarkable fur, but she's cleaner than a cat.
Nostrils on the top of her nose,
she can breathe through a pile of leaves,
and just about anything nourishes her and her brood.

She's been on the main marquee
since the continents floated apart.
But nocturnal and arboreal,
you don't see her clearly
until you think she's dead.

She's just lying there lying,
waiting for the hiatus
wherein you go to get a shovel
while she wends her way back to herself and
her little stroll out of your life.

Sheena, Queen of the Jungle, Lived

Sheena, Queen of the Jungle, lived
in my neighborhood,
across the street and down the way
from my girlfriend's family

so I always knew
the Africa of B movie fame
wasn't anything like life at all.

Nobody African ever ran around
on ground as flat as a sound stage
or jumped in and out of hokey-pokey
sagebrush bushes wearing a grass skirt.

To know truth from fiction this way
is the legacy of growing up in North Hollywood
which is not quite Hollywood
except in the imagination of people
who have never been there.

North Hollywood is where the people live
who paint the sets and set the toupees,
who make the rain fall and the snow bank,
make the bullets pock the sides of buildings
and blow out the backs of the bad guys
so that the cloth of their pinstripe suits
puckers like little bottle-cap kisses.

People who live in North Hollywood
replace the spun sugar bottles on the tables
after each take of the barroom brawls.
They drive the Honey Wagons
and late into the night deliver
rewrites to houses in the canyons—
one color for the script revision today,
another color tomorrow and on and on.

North Hollywood's a short drive
over the pass from Tinseltown.
It sits snug up against Burbank's
military industrial Quonset huts
where the dykes on the line at Lockheed
built the Starfighters,
bolted down the passenger seats
of the L1011's, and played a little pool
in a couple of low-down bars about two blocks
from where Sheena, Queen of the Jungle,
really did walk around her backyard
in leopard skin lingerie,
and her hair was blonde, truly blonde,
and it was rumored
she occasionally did swing from her trees.

Hommage

Here's who we fucked our brains out for
one night in Paris 2002—
once for Natalie Barney, once for Renee Vivian,
twice for monogamous Gertrude and Alice,
then again for Djuna Barnes and Romaine Brooks
(as we never would for Hemingway because he couldn't take a joke
and never for poor Jim Morrison who really is dead as a lizard),
and then for Colette and all her *jeune filles*
and the splendid sacrifice of Liane de Pougy
and who knows how many times
for Rosa Bonheur in the countryside
with her menagerie

Lessons of a Saturday Afternoon

A boy and unaware,
so natural in his grace

that Socrates would have sighed
to see him,

is washing a car
in the driveway next to mine.

He does not know.
Sometimes he bends just so—it is ballet

and a new muscle shows,
then he trips on nothing

and he goes
from protection to desire in me.

So soon, I am old enough
to love a boy.

Tripod Dog

Three-legged dog
at the Bierhaus in Mytilene.
Sappho, at the table
next to the amp
notes that the three-legged dog
seen scrounging
in the grass at Atlantic Market
has made his way
with a pack of ten
into the Bierhaus for
New Year's Eve dinner and party.

And the Blond Bitch Goddess
who strides in with her two daughters,
floor-length fur coats flying,
high-stepping to their table
in front of the fireplace,
draws every island eye.

New Year's Eve and the Tripod Dog
lounging outside the ladies' room
leaps up to snag my arm.
A shepherd-mix barks
and romps around the revelers
while wiry terriers
and plump mixed-breed Poms
tug and tussle for table scraps.

Beware of the pack
that forms in the wild,
sends blood to bloodlet
and starts the deadly chase.

Oh, where to go?—to the dark
precincts of the
Three-legged Dog

or the blond night of the Bierhaus
and society of the human kind
with its island hierarchies
and clans kissing the hands
of other clans

while in the new born year the
surface of the harbor
rings with rain

Flower Shop

Stepping in from the street,
the heat would drop away
and a sigh of greenery
announce itself.

First it was "Bill's Flowers" lettered in blue
on the window and the white panel truck.
Bill was a blond model-type,
something short of 6 feet tall
and skinny in a tight jeans kind of way.

And then he was gone. Men were dying
overnight, it seemed, from some new death blow
eventually named AIDS. Did Bill ever look sick?
Who knew what to look for,
we were just shopping for flowers.

It was a place to order up a special bouquet,
pink *Heliconia* or white ginger blossoms, maybe.
Thai orchards with sweet baby faces,
pricey but spectacular. Always something
exotic highlighting the beautiful window displays.

Paul took over after Bill died. The truck got repainted
with a little pinstripe below the name "Paul's Plants".
I was buying more vases and single stems of things.
I liked to wander from room to room,
the best part of shopping there,
moving through the flower shop's damp and tactile air.

Now Paul is dead, too—his meds never worked.
The truck reads "Green & Co."
Letters in a ceramic lime,
and right at the end of the line,
two little daisies punctuating it.

I don't know Green yet. Maybe he's a survivor.
Maybe he's young. He's pretty great, though,
with the window displays. My friend Maria
thinks he has a background in set design.
All of the workers have stayed on and so has
a chill in that beautiful glade of rooms.

Because I Was A Girl, For Christ's Sake

Once in high school I pitched a no-hitter,
and during the post-game interview at 3rd base,
the field lights turning off
and cars pulling away from Olive Rec,
the reporter asked me if
I knew what a no-hitter was.

I shifted my weight.
My cleats crunched
on the chalk line.
I could feel the
sweat and dirt
drying on my face.
I wanted to leave and meet my friends,
but my boyfriend
wanted me to leave with him
after the interview.

"You're a girl, for Christ's sake, " he had said,
You're coming with me."

My Sapphic Heritage

time over time
//

double am

I am

//
double you

forward to me

//
all the nerves shine

So The Teacher Jumped Up On The Desk

So the teacher jumped up on the desk
in our Freshman English class,
the front door to the mind for us little less than
middle-class Catholic girls at Immaculate Heart College &,
our eyes fixed on our professor, his spit flying,
his suit coat and tie flying,
him waving a little black & white copy of this *Howl*
like it's a hymnal and & he's got religion,
he's got the juju chant & rattle
of a million dead rosaries sent electrical
shock to revive & turn themselves into the
knuckle joints and knee bones of the living—
Let's dance it all started to say, let's
shake this thing, this hour, this book, this life
which is not going to be the one you registered
for—NO, you are not going to return to the
parish & iron the altar cloths. NO, you are not
going to carpool, learn golf, play bridge
on Tuesdays or join the Catholic Daughters
of America, you are NOT going to make
Jell-O molds & tat doilies, you are going
to smoke a lot of dope & waste the weekends
drinking gallons of Gallo Hearty Burgundy
shirtless on the patio and you won't be alone.
The Beatles are coming, the Beatles are coming &
you are getting a booster shot for anti-war proclivities,
you are getting so amped that language
will not rest like a four-cylinder low-mileage
car in your garage but turn into a nitro-burning

dragster in your guts—peeling, wheeling, weaving
from lane to lane before abandoning the pavement
altogether, airborne without a parachute.
You are ready for *flame out flame out.*
The sky opening like a mouth & wrapping its lips
around your paganized shoeless and blessed feet says
inhale the impetus to flee your former self,
ditch all your classes & go who knows where
or cares.

Greek Rhythm With Greens

Balsamic vinegar & strong greens,
the Barbitos and its bursts of song for
Our Lady of the Wayside Mutts
and Broken Branches,
Our Lady of the Fervent Kiss
and Clasp of Hands.

Here's easy tears
as the musicians
signal each other
during a song.

Off we go—eight bars
more.

The Lady of Mechanical
Necessities—change
of oil, change of
belts—oh, my Blessed Lady
of Inevitable Processes,
I light my lamp to you,
light the candles
and sing before
the candles flare out.
Here's a cake for the
camshaft &
here's a cake for
the karaoke dreamer,

I can't stop
loving you,
I've made up
my mind.

And here's to you, Lady of El Valle.
Another year cycles around
and the three-legged dog
takes a nap in the hallway

next to the ladies
room door New Year's Eve.

Chant a suitable ending
to the year,
chant the magic ritual
for the next.
Nail my enemies'
balls to the wall
on the magic lead sheet
of curses.

In the wildwood,
Artemis gathers
her pack,
whistles,
wakes the Tripod Dog
and heads again
for the hills.

Recipe with Dogs

Dogs, out of the kitchen!—repeated five times in ascending notes
and increasing volume as the hands sweep through the air
with or without cooking implement or towel.

Don't drop anything because a dog will dart into the kitchen
and you will have to repeat step one and increase the volume
and perhaps even make a threat or two, step briskly toward them,

or if something does fall in front of the sink, a dog will dive
and get her/his nose under the lip of the cabinet
and maybe let out a yelly yelp

which is pretty much meaningless
in the lifetime of two dogs who are waiting at the edge
of the tile for the cook to turn her back and shift her

attention to the REAL recipe, the one with at least
a countertop full of leafy things with fronds drooping
where a skillful dog can reach and run from the room

with cilantro, kale, beet tops, anything green and gorgeous
anything that feels like a precursor to a real meal like that breast,
of chicken unswaddled from its Saran wrap and pretty slippery

right now, pretty "possible" in the mind of a dog whose owner
is reaching into the cupboard, back turned, humming a tune
and not quite as mindful as she should be, silly believer

in what she just said for the three millionth time
in the life of these two canines—like they care
about repetition, maybe being reincarnations

of those kitchen loving poodles Gertrude Stein
used to spoil with little treats and little oppsy-dipsy pets,
little smoochy-mouth French words

that are even now taking our minds off the fact
the dogs are in the kitchen again and the cook
is back to step one, screaming, "Dogs!! Out of the kitchen!!

Working Towards Sappho

I

I can't always be sure I'm getting anywhere.
Maybe the clue is in the way Mytilene streets
drive toward the city center through
the stack and sprawl of squared off stones,
the one-way lanes and round-abouts.

I have to live in so many minds
to talk to Sappho about the books of law
that stand between us,
the Bible and the Koran,
books that rule a world
she knew nothing about.

And me, not knowing much of her,
not even knowing what "news"
meant in her life, what exile meant
and how she knew to leave the island
and if it was night or day when she fled.

Her approvals//the beautiful women.
But what fruit did she put on her table?

Invite Sappho and me into the same room
and what would we talk about?

She wouldn't know someone had walked
on the moon.
I wouldn't know whether she had a dog.

What did it mean to say what she said
in 600 BCE?

How did she feel about
her own beauty? Hints

she didn't make,
or they're missing.

The only through line
is the erotic charge around women

and that she loved her life

II

Would there be room in Lesvos
for Sappho now?

Little shrines along the roads
in the form of miniature churches
are stuffed with empty bottles
and cans of beer.

In the cafes, men talking, men loudly
talking to other men
in rooms that boom
with the voices of men
talking to men,
smoking and drinking.
Would there be room for her voice
in the overlay of sounds
of the men filling every vessel?

From shrine to church to altar,
their images are pounded into icons
and the Infant Christ sits like a squalling ham
in the Virgin's lap.

III

The Villa of the Papyri at Herculaneum, containing the library of Lucius Calpurnius Piso Caesoninus, Julius Caesar's father-in-law, was preserved by the eruption of Mount Vesuvius, but has only been partially excavated.

Another poet in another time
might live her lesbian life
with other facts
that come to light
in the unearthing of the library
at Herculaneum.

Down from antiquity, untouched
by the monks of the Middle Ages,
hundreds of carbonized scrolls burned and buried
by the eruption of Vesuvius,
now await their translators.

What could be found there?
Affirmation of Sappho's life as we know it,
or something entirely different?

Whatever emerges, a poem
written by a lesbian poet
has a heritage of flame,
and no matter what Sappho was,
any woman who "comes out"
springs from a burned life
as a poem.

IV

I can't know if Sappho
would understand
all the facets of my life.
I've lived with one woman
for almost twenty years.
We're not alone in this.

But I believe Sappho would understand
the moment when one woman
has been circling the other
for an hour or so,
a look in her manner
tense and vulnerable.

Sappho would put down
whatever instrument
was in her hands
and go to her.

This is the moment and the bond that begs
affirmation.

This is the rest of the story
writing itself among us.

The future must bristle with the names of women
like fragrant cloves in an orange,
like quills on a healthy porcupine,
like hexagonal columns of basalt
that rise from the earth
and cool in the shape of cathedral naves.

It can be known, it has been written, it can't be changed.

What I Would Want To Know

after viewing the Peplos Kore (Acropolis / about 530 BCE)

What I would want
to know

is
what's involved

in taking off
your clothes

For The Girl Child

She who was told small and smaller,
told less and be quiet,

she who was told change or be changed,
has stood by her own side

this whole time it has taken
to break the telling and its iron hold

over her muscles, to heal the strain
and the strangeness of her own disavowed body.

See now, she has grown stronger
than the strength it took
to keep her small.

When Did A Self Begin?

(for my mother Carmen V. Klein, 1922-2006)

I

Eared wheat, silky corn, squash blossoms
at the bulbous end of a squash, that vegetable umbilical
squirreling through the garden, around the gate post,
its tendrils like ringlets of a green god rising and twining.

This is what I know from childhood,
pictures in my mind for growth.
I could add the animals straying in their pastures
or stolid in pens in the farmyard,
or the daily industry of egg laying in the chicken house
and the chickens pecking in the dirt.

Where did a self begin then?
Not to speak of me, but her.
Hair cut straight across her forehead
in photographs, hungry eyes.
Even now they say hunger, but not as deep and dark.

II

Childhood in rural South Dakota.
Rough row, everybody says it.
If you didn't grind and till and plow,
and even if you did and the rain didn't come
or spring frost killed the shoots,
if the food didn't come up
out of the ground,
you starved.

But her great-grandfather kept the eggs
to give to the plow horses for their coats.
What economy of scale explains this?
Her own mother, sickly all her life
and dead at age fifty of leukemia,
most often a childhood disease.

Where did my mother begin, then?
In scarcity, in the dry rows at the edge
of the cornfield where the watermelons
lay heartless after pillage. The boys from town
or the tramps on their way to the river taking the best.

Each younger sister taking something away.
Time spent untangling the curls of the sister
who cheated and the sister who lied.
Cooking the one steak for the sick mother
who grew up on bacon grease sandwiches
carried to school in the small black tin.

My mother's father at the tractor yelling
as she began to turn over the engine,
"Be the boy in the family."

She the one yelled at most,
made of other people's demands.
Nightly fearing the sleepwalking sister
would tumble down the stairs
and she be blamed,
though more often than not
the sister was found in the morning
covered with quilts in the bathtub.

III

Measured against the river undercutting the bank,
what force would be the one to point to?
The swelling tide of a small family
or war and disease and three children
to raise during hard times?

What river cut the bank out,
left no island, instead a tearing away of soil,
the sound of deep roots separating
from the flat planet of prairie and sailing away?

I learned to fear standing too close to the river
out there in the pasture, the car left running
while the grownups walked to the edge
to watch the flood carving a new river bed,
knowing the wet hollows would spring
with mushrooms, that hundreds of pale heads
would rise from the mysterious spoon-like depressions
where rocks had rolled away
in the current and downstream.

They were the other children of the floodtide,
drowned and drowned again forever.

That swamped and silent life
leaving its impressions, its shadows like thumbprints.
Identity flowing onward, then gone by, forever gone by.

IV

There were vast monochromes she could stare into,
horizontal beiges stacking like lines of muted music
if she could but reach to hear it over the constant wind.
The striated sky lowering until the horizon disappeared
and the tornado clouds came up, the birds silent,
animals huddling in the corner of the field,
the lowest place where the creek shoveled under
the barbed wire fence, the grey posts
with their roots hanging free of their tether to earth.

Then more wind, blocks of blue-black chunks
like slate stacking and twirling,
like the way she starts to think—a habit of mind
that's a confusion of ends and means—
sky gone dark to storm and swirl,
stunned there like the plains tipping on their axis into night.
Then little stars stabbing through, stuttering for hours
across the great black flatness after wind.

Her aunt, once picked up in a tornado and flown a mile,
had cornstalks driven through her ears.
She could hear only through the soles of her feet.
Cars and trains sang up her calves. She would sway
side to side, reach a hand out to someone,
a problem with balance besides the silence.
That story was told me by my mother
when as a child I met my great aunt
and we all posed for a photo—four generations,
north, east, south, and west—
and me down there in the corner
close to the paper anchor that held the picture
fast to the page.

V

The summer sweltering, Main Street a stew
of wavy heat steaming up from the pavement
and the road tar melting mid-day.
She sways in the restaurant kitchen and stumbles
to the counter where a man catches her.
Someone runs to get dad at the Ford garage.

I am nowhere to be found, down by the creek
with Tiny and Big Boy and Carol, digging crayfish
out of the mud. It isn't hot down in the culvert.
We only know how hot it is
when I get home and she is down
on the bed with an ice bag on her head.

Heat stroke, that's what they say.
She comes to, looking like she took a punch,
but rises at the bell next morning for work,
dips a handkerchief in ice water
and ties it around her neck.
Calcium deficiency, the doctor declared.

What did the heat heap on her then?
A knock-out, dad says, just like when Rocky Marciano,
pale as a chef's uniform, knocked out the champ,
Joe Louis. Hard to fathom for a seven-year old
that your mother could fall over in the middle of the day.

VI

Under the anesthetic, she dies
into the hands of another and returns,
the gases in her blood crossing
back to the proportion and balance
of the living. I sit like a scribe
in the outer chamber waiting room
while her soul comes back
into the wrapper. Keeping track
is my ordinary task, doing some work
while I worry how she will make her way back
into the stitched and bolted frame of her body.

She was somebody more and less new
after each of her fourteen surgeries.
She begins again in a different pose.
One time she cannot turn her head
more than 40 degrees off-center,
one time she cannot lower her chin
enough to see her feet and forever after
she returns to a clever trap, her body,
which she must elude in sleep or dreams.
The question is, did she ever fully come back
into the moving world again?

VII

Into a ceramic grid of snow-white tile,
she falls face first onto the bathroom floor
in the retirement home.
She falls toward a blankness she lives in
for some months, her face maroon
from forehead down to her mouth,
a waterfall of blood inside the skin

She doesn't remember it.

Nor does she remember a white rush of opiates
whiplashing out of her body
from the wrong dose of morphine.
Nor the five paramedics who carried her
out of the house and into the ambulance,
her yelling, "He's not dead,
he'll come for me. He's somewhere
just down the street, my husband, Ray."

When I first saw her in the emergency room,
she was a gauze-trussed mummy,
shaking as if she had been plugged
into the 12 volt outlet on the way to the hospital.

VIII

"Your mother has died."

That's the phone call I'm always waiting for,
but it could be the boy crying wolf.
The good shepherd, the bad boy, the bad shepherd,
the good boy, the beneficent wolf.

Then, I'm in Ohio and the standby doctor
from intensive care calls about her DNR.

"The language is confusing," he says, "what does she want?"
I have a voice for this, the good daughter on top of things.
We have talked it over and over. She has bought her plot
and she told me casket closed. I'm ok with it all, I'm ok,
but ever waiting for the next call, the one for "next of kin".

I'm ready for this. Herself without me in the rain
of grief I'm in. Herself, can she begin again?
Can she find the door to a next life
swinging open, can she settle into
a better body next time?

I wish her one that has a full and happy laugh,
the one I heard when I was twelve, when on my birthday
she and my aunt got drunk and sang "Sweet Georgia Brown"
but never did that kind of crazy thing again.

IX

Crazy, a word with angles in it and letters
that can get you far away. Cracking noises
and a sharp buzz. I look in her mouth and see
her bottom teeth and her jaw set. She's gone
into another spin and now it sets in,
reminding me of my aunt, that day she came into our yard,
her hair a Brillo halo crackling with blue sparks,
her eyes whirling into space and back again.
She was drunk or crazy,
and those were pretty much the choices.

It terrified me to see my mother's face
could get that look, angry and white,
spraying spit and foam,
her voice a corridor of gravel and ice,
"Come here, come here, come here."

Daily life is a wheel and all it ever means
has rolled on past. Hallucinations replace it.
The dead come in and out of my mother's room.
Chickens crowd the Post Office. Don't I see them?
What's wrong with me then? She screams
to make sure someone hears her—"what's wrong with *me*?"

X

May 2004 and all the nurses and doctors on 2 East
have known this woman a month.

Six months ago she was my mother.
They didn't know her then,

the one busy in the crafts room
painting ceramic Christmas trees by the dozen.

Nobody had made the terrible mistakes with her meds.

They think she's the woman in 250 C who screams
"help me right now," who falls out of the bed each night

and, well, forget it, I tell myself. Tenth life for this cat,
and god bless her and who she will be next.

XI

3:20 in the morning.

I know on the first ring she's gone,
snuck out in the middle of the night
and died without me there.

When we arrive at the hospital
my mother is lying quiet as a mouse.
I stroke her brow, and kiss her hands and cry
and put my head on the rails of the bed.

This is the old body I know so well,
and the day, and the day, and the day
that was coming.

Two weeks ago she stopped
eating and drinking and speaking.
The nurses say it's common, the person decides.

XII

Last week on the "Days Gone By" page
of my home town paper, *The Remsen Bell-Enterprise*,
a snapshot from 1948.
My grandparents are off to Luxembourg.
At the train depot, family and friends pose.
I have no memory of this event,
but when I see the photo I cry anyway.

My mother, the living one,
stands in the front row.
She's holding somebody's baby in one arm
and has me by the hand.
My hair is blond and I'm wearing long pants
under my winter coat.

Oh, I know this muse-child
standing so close to her mother,
the dreamy smile and expectant look.
I will always be her only child,
though I don't have a clue yet what it will mean.
Later I realize it's a life's work, that love.

That mother, this child.

The Dry Air of Egypt

Sappho did not know herself
the way we know her, a piece
or two, saved by the dry air of Egypt.

She knew herself
on a green island
with music and song,

with bountiful bays and boats
setting out at dawn,
sea winds at night.

She knew herself
minute by minute, and
on to the next

line, on to the next
note, touch, smile,
lamp to be lit.

Whole, or something like
how we know ourselves
right now, this breath and the next.

"A Text of Broken Texts"

—Page DuBois, *Sappho Is Burning*

Under every river is the floor of the world,
and curling downstream a beautiful ribbon
printed with the story
of where water comes from and returns.

Under the sea is the mother of the world
and from her fiery body islands appear
and begin their march away
from their birth ground,
spangled dots above the waves.

From cliffs and shores, I've seen many islands,
sister and brother islands,
across a rocking plain of water.

Long sweeps of waves mark their beaches
like brush strokes, leaving a hint at the tide line
of a poem taken back into the body
of the sea time and time again.

Who speaks for anything? Who can hold
the paper or the brush long enough?
Is not everything we know a little island
set off from something larger,
a shoreline to walk while thinking,
while imagining?

Doesn't every story begin ankle-deep in the sea?

Rites

I

This is the body

   bloated   bruised

blistered   racked

ruined

and again the mouth

     that has kissed and laughed,

where language,

     that first spring of sound,

burbled

II

The priest comes with the prayer book,
the oil, the bread,
but he comes to my mother
who cannot raise her head
or open her eyes.

We stand on the dry cliff of her life
and he begins to pray.
The book is scalloped
where his fingers have so often
run down the side of each page.
As he reads, where he touches the paper
to turn it, there is a little wave of wear.

III

I am trying to remember
my days in her body
when she was young
and wanting this baby to come.
I have known her longer than my life.

IV

Bruised, those lips that kissed the world.

Her eyes shut, her breathing scraping

like a shovel on dry earth.

The words of the priest and the prayers,

also dry, reminiscent of the stillness

in a church, parishioners standing as one,

dark coats in winter, finery at the feast days,

But, I say that under all this, my body prays

its own prayers and will not

obey the rhetoric of the celibate man.

V

Once in the garden,
everything was green.

Anything she put into the ground
grew unceasingly.

VI

Remember, mother, the devotion you had
was always to Her, the mother, too.

The mother-tongue aching against
the roof and root of the mouth,
that was me. The little denizen of the book.

VII

Amen, amen to everything.
The wing, yes, amen to that blue thing,
amen to the porch, the tree, the shop.

Amen to me, to you, to dad,
to that blissful sister who died on you,
and her son who died, too.

Amen to sweet cakes, wet clay,
branches of the brambling hedge
and the paint brush drying on the table.

Amen to knowing you
will always know me and my motives.
Amen to all of us who were *us* for years.

We sit at the end of the day with a book.
Who cares what it says or who reads it?
Who cares what the title is? We read it
and when we are done, it never is done, thank god.

VIII

The lonely priest, retired from all the priestly jobs:
the bitter Stations of the Cross,
the holy oils, the guilty confessions

of the sad penitents. Bless all of them
who stay and all of them who leave.
Bless us all for how duration and durable

and stone
mean
the same thing in the end.

Not Disappearing

The poems I write
to you, Sappho,
seem bird-bone light
in comparison
to my poems about cars
and the freeway
and the heavy-metal centuries
in which I've lived.

Something disappears
when I talk to you,
and it also happens
that each word's history
leads to a question—

what nouns and verbs
could we share
straight up?

I think the most beautiful words
are drifting, smoky things
with such long histories
you would have known them
as I know them:

dawn,
the moon,
waves and boats,
laurel trees.

I think we both know the meaning
of a line of women walking
back from the beach,
some singing, some
carrying baskets—
and one who runs ahead,
runs not in a direct line,
but dips like a swallow—

and a cloudless pale blue sky.

Biographical Note

Eloise Klein Healy is the author of *Building Some Changes* (Beyond Baroque Foundation NewBook Award), *A Packet Beating Like A Heart* (rara avis), *Ordinary Wisdom* (Paradise Press/reissued by Red Hen Press), *Women's Studies Chronicles* (The Inevitable Press Chapbook Series), *Artemis In Echo Park* (Firebrand Books), *Passing* (Red Hen Press), and three spoken word recordings.

Her work is frequently anthologized in collections such as *Another City: Writing From Los Angeles*; *California Poetry: From The Gold Rush To The Present*; *Intimate Nature: The Bond Between Women and Animals*; *Grand Passion: Poets of Los Angeles and Beyond*; *The Geography Of Home: California's Poetry of Place*; and *The World In Us: Lesbian and Gay Poetry of the Next Wave*. She has been awarded residencies at The MacDowell Colony and Dorland Arts Colony and fellowships from The California Arts Council, California State University Northridge, and a COLA Fellowship from the City of Los Angeles. Healy was the Founding Chair of the MFA in Creative Writing Program at Antioch University Los Angeles. She directed the Women's Studies Program at California State University Northridge and taught in the Feminist Studio Workshop at The Woman's Building in Los Angeles. Currently, she is a Guest Poet at the Idyllwild Summer Poetry Festival.

Healy is co-founder of ECO-ARTS, an eco-tourism/arts venture and founding editor of ARKTOI, an imprint of Red Hen Press. She received the Horace Mann Award from Antioch University Los Angeles where she is Distinguished Professor of Creative Writing Emerita.